THE TOWER.

The Tower

Paul Legault

Coach House Books, Toronto

first edition

Published with the generous assistance of the Canada Council for the Arts and the Ontario Arts Council. Coach House Books also acknowledges the support of the Government of Canada through the Canada Book Fund.

LIBRARY AND ARCHIVES CANADA CATALOGUING IN PUBLICATION

Title: The tower / Paul Legault.
Names: Legault, Paul, 1985- author.
Description: Poems.
Identifiers: Canadiana (print) 20200158872 | Canadiana (ebook) 20200158899 | ISBN 9781552454114 (softcover) | ISBN 9781770566415 (EPUB) | ISBN 9781770566422 (PDF)
Classification: LCC PS3612.E47T69 2020 | DDC 811/.6—dc23

The Tower is available as an ebook: ISBN 978 1 77056 641 5 (EPUB) and ISBN 978 1 77056 642 2 (PDF)

Purchase of the print version of this book entitles you to a free digital copy. To claim your ebook of this title, please email sales@chbooks.com with proof of purchase. (Coach House Books reserves the right to terminate the free digital download offer at any time.)

For George Hyde-Lees

For Joseph Kaplan

CONTENTS

SAILING TO BYZANTIUM AGAIN

1.

This country's too young to think – beyond beauty
and public sex. Like birds or people,
dying's gotten old. Yes, please,
like these thousands of mermen teeming upstream
   to marry,
like how blood oranges and pot generate summer,
flood my bed with an assortment of gold-plated iPhones
that they may represent the dead and this living
in a prosperous age fully loaded.

2.

Old people are like Pokémon.
They were free once before the civil wars
they waged inside Time, which is an imaginary country
of which they're refugees. There are
training grounds for love in America
and virtually everywhere. They're handheld,
so hold mine on a speedboat full of blow on our way
to the idea of 1990s Miami in your mind that I whisper
   to you called *Byzantium*.

3.

O minor celebs and major arcana
like vortices of yourselves blowing up endlessly,
burn through this glass wall, look Western,
and be what the soul follows like an addict of
the substance of the heart. You should always
be absorbing that animal fact that 💀
you could just as easily
be transformed into a pigeon
as an owl as a dream as not.

4.

When I become posthuman, I'll probably still read
poems about the human experience, if only
because their unnaturally formed connections
help get me off-track. Sleepy god,
dissolve like a song or a tablet
into champagne in your crowd of high priestesses.
Then sing that this is itself that sung thing
of what was holy, or is, or's gonna be.

THE TOWER

1.

How will I do being old when I'm old –
having to use this same heart in its place.
Tell all my cells to be made of me younger,
Madonna. I won't budge until time makes me
          do it. God likes getting older
like an animal who escaped from the zoo
only to visit on Sundays with her children.
I never had a tail to chase.
I got bored in Plato's cave,
which is to say I was young and stupid.
Once I've worn the imagined world out
like a cheap wig, conquered heaven
with you as my bride, Imagination,
give it up and finally teach me the hack
that lets you convert abstraction into life:
more of it. Or, fuck, just spill over,
heavy glass, as the fly caught under you flies off –

2.

– and onto my pale finger. I feel
like a Brita filter in the rain.
You make me want more stuff
like puppies and the heaven we make
of this feeling of getting things wildly in order
for once, because once we start
things stop – then don't ever do that.
Kissing you is like asking the trees

to say something, and then they actually do,
they say *TREES*. Reflective surface,
I leave it to you to report any news
of what's coming up from behind me reliably.
I'm generally disturbed
by the golden age of television, but I also feel
like I do about everything a little:
I like it. Let it come at me

like Sarah Paulson de-eyeing herself
in *American Horror Story: Coven*
so she can truly see
(because the last time she went blind,
before Frances Conroy gave her a new pair
of regular eyes, after she lost them,
she could receive visions from the past.
But it doesn't work twice, until later it does

and she sees me watch her see me).
I'd like to get to know the future a little first
before going all the way. Things are constantly
things and constantly saying *Let us happen*,
so we can increase as a culture. Something
is always letting itself happen.
Calling it culture makes it sound dirty.
These new forces rise with or without

a target audience. Whatever you give,
give a shit, or you'll be descended upon
by a pigeon or a vulture. There aren't always
too many birds. C'mere, falconress,
I'm whistling at you. Good luck coming down
from your beautiful sky, Mr. Bones.
I say let's you and me GTFO of here.
How many mysteries does it take to make a season

like spring? Who's texting me this late?
Why did I have that dream that my water broke?
Why's time still a thing?
I learned how to make croissants on the internet.
I am comforted by the meanderings of the crowd.
I hear Canadian geese are pests, but all I hear
when I think of them is *honk*.
Fly Away Home is the new *Wild Swans at Coole*.

Anna Paquin is the new Maud Gonne. She was good
in *Castle in the Sky*, the way an imaginary friend is:
as a disembodied voice. In *Angel*,
Angel takes the sewer tunnels.
I'm bad at avoiding the sun.
All different kinds of light are light.
Blind people are better at writing poetry.
The best thing I can do is make you crazy.

I remember when all that mattered was that
Helen fell in love. Baby, you make me
get this way. Luckily, it's my favourite
way out. The Trojans got around
just fine until they didn't, until they did
again when they won the 2004 championship,
until the BCS stripped them of their national title
for using drugs, like that's the worst thing

they ever did. I don't think I'd want to kill
an army of people for love, but I love you
enough to ride inside a horse, at full gallop,
into your city, via the upper level
of the George Washington Bridge. New York,
you look all your gift horses in the trunk.
When I was on the island, I learned to hunt
for the best food in hidden places.

I used to sit on the edge of the highest building
and look down to see what everyone was wearing

so I could know if I should borrow your denim jacket
or somebody else's umbrella. If *Spiderman* can be
a musical, then I can be a Spiderman.
For my audition on *The Voice*, I'm going to sing
'Yes, I'm a Witch' by Yoko Ono in slow motion
and wait for the chairs to turn around.

Shakira and Rihanna walk into a club
and forget everything. I can't usually remember
what day it is, unless there's a festival.
I want to be naked as you at The Country Club
in NOLA in April in nothing but your birthday
suit and tie with me, wet as a two-dollar rental towel.
But now it's the fifteenth, and I haven't paid my taxes,
but I've started to. The blood moon eclipse

is really happening; it's not a metaphor,
though it stranges things like one does.
Everything's a little Cormac-McCarthyish.
It's zero degrees Celsius, and I just walked over
an actual bed of magnolia blossoms.
There was ice on the car mirror.
The birds are being insane.
It's four in the morning,

and their insanity is a sound,
since I can't see them. Thankfully,
they're not speaking to me in Greek;
the crazy hasn't spread but is nonetheless

indicative of the landscape's instability.
Laganja Estranja, I am not your momma.
Just do you but be careful: if you do
you too often, it's sickening.

3.

I've never written a will.
I leave everything to myself
but specifically the version of myself
that's something else, like a Siri.
So you can ask: *Paul,*
where is the best pizza?
And I can say: *New York.*
Have you seen *Ghostwriter*?
I hear Smiley's used to serve
a 'special slice,' with anchovies
and a packet of coke. I guess they did
so they could leave something behind
for their pizza-boys and pizza-daughters.
Who's to say I've no heirs?
There you are! You, reading this,
summoning my pride. If you don't
know you by now, now's your chance.
Exhibit your inhibitions in a glass
enclosure. Have yours blown
into a transparent life-sized replica of you.
Put a message in your human-shaped bottle
like: *Hey*, or, *¡Ayúdame!* or
This letter is from the future ...
Don't let the moment not happen.
My return won't e-file. I feel like a
honkytonk woman. I feel like
the invisible layer of glass that separates us

from our past is bulletproof. Every time
I see a bullethole in a window, I want to put my finger in it.
The whole place is rigged to blow in less than ten minutes.
There's some kind of emergency override,
but it might be best to just ride this one out
naked on a horse on a beach in Spain.
If I ever get decimated by an asteroid,
my nephew, Paul Legault, can be me
when I've gone ahead and become whatever.
But I bequeath the operator's manual to all y'all.
Manually speaking, I use my mouth.
Textually, I'm attempting to use what I sound like
when you read this inside of your head
as a way of saying: *Hello,*
I want to sound
like a bird's sleepy cry
among the shades,
like one shady bitch.

My superpower is all mirrors
and luck. Don't break them.
Seven years is like infinity in that
I don't know them yet.
One must be oneself
and what said self does,
but there's a loophole.

If the poet does not use her powers,
beauty goes on using them anyway

for her own purposes. Someone just yelled
fag twice out of their car window, one for me
and one for this other guy in an argyle vest,
who I now assume is gay – he probably is.
I have an iced coffee and a new haircut.
We make blank expressions at each other.

It is the gentlest of muggings:
thought turned to language
like Rimbaud turned to crime.
I'm going to send my soul to Harvard,
so it can drop out, then start Weezer,
then go back to finish its degree later.
It pulled the red string when I walked away.
It was God in the Fire with His Revolver.
I never really wanted to have a clue
about what being dead is like,
but there's this dead rabbit
on the side of the road
my dog apparently wants to eat.
There's sleep and how birds do that.
There's cloud storage.

MEDITATIONS IN TIME OF DISASTER

1. MTV Cribs

There has to be an MTV crib
nestled in the Hills like a bunny
into its nest where life keeps on
making it rain, spilling blow underwater
just to prove a point. Neptune's like: Y'all,
this is how we roll in the middle of it –
space cowboys lost interdimensionally,
separate from no lie but the truth.

Dream a little; don't jump from the boat.
That's the good advice that didn't take.
Hart Crane, you fishy bitch, come to me
comfortably, like a man inside an image
of gold fruit, sequined pyramids, glass storms,
ancestrally, stern as a boss in a merger.
What were your grandparents like,
and who did your great-grandparents do –

powerful as ghosts when you don't think of them?
We all have to take better care of the dead world
like in *The Vampire Diaries* how Bonnie does that.
I never really liked what they told you to do
just the way sometimes they said it beautifully.
Prune the seaweed in your vodka pool
so we can serve hand-rolls on the piazza

off my freshly cleaned body like in one
of those places where they re-enact the past
as portrayed by poorly paid actors, in this case
to depict what happened in the early twenty-first century
when capitalism is entirely belated.
I guess people have been eating food
off each other's bodies since the world
existed with people in it. Forever
is such a fun thing to keep trying to describe.

I'd like to do it that way: forever.
Talk dirty to me about the future. Lick the mic.
This is a judgement-free zone.
Hey girlfriend, what is the fuck-up?
Life gets so caught up. Still-life, spill a little
bit of the wine. Shift your jewellery

next to mine because we're going
to realize what we're seeing stood still
like a planet you never heard of
that just stopped like now like how
it ain't even a thing. Fag is as fag does.
Whose job is it to mine the disorder
if not us poetcetera? Here's the thing
that ain't. What if how pretty buildings are

makes you sad? They say go to the woods
or else just be more woodsy in the capital.
Pine in my direction in the pines.

Construct a feminine mystique like Gaia,
like you could really fuck me up
if you wanted to. Tornadoes and things
like drought or too much sunlight are
nature's more charming powers of destruction

2. My House

The Sun's going to have an apocalypse first.
I'm comforted to know that one person knows
everything about it. I forget what her name is.
I looked up 'The Sun' too long on Wikipedia.
It does have a Twitter account, @TheSun.
I couldn't think of anything to say to it.
How is there anything so almost perfectly
spherical and consisting of hot plasma
interwoven with magnetic fields that gets
everywhere, that says everywhere:

You are my people? It is their symbol
of life. Ours too. I've never been to the tundra,
but I hear some people even like it there.
The Sun told me that. Also,
Kurma, the tortoise that is the world,
is divided into twenty-seven lunar mansions –
all of which are for rent.
They say there's this possibility in asking.
I think I was born in the wrong part. How do
I say that in the form of a question?

I don't own a house. Homer's home
run goes: run home, Odysseus,
(the price of home a rocket in the sky)
or wander like a pirate turned pilot
turned back or vice versa.

What else is there to say:
all art seems monument to something
sweeter than life that exists in it separate
from the body, blah, blah, blah –
except by saying that this isn't?

3. My Windows

I have two feelings and a bust
of my own head. You touch it,
and somehow I get the sliver.
Nonsense lies somewhere beyond
the window sill where I placed my tail
like a weapon I plan to regenerate later.
I'm listening harder than usual.
It's like summer school but sexier.
Some asshole thinks he's Picasso again.
Some love is modern, some's post-that.
Up on the roof, the Drifters keep drifting –
up, probably, and into the sky.
Take good care of my baby. Blue
never looked good on her. It wasn't her
colour. She didn't own it yet.
She could still listen to the blues and think
they sound pretty
like a weekend. I've got one of those.
Let's fill it with cash.
Your dragon ain't my dragon,
but I'm gonna ride it.
You're rarer than a heart
before it's been cooked.
Like some diamonds lost
when we went jet-skiing,
you're naked as the sea in the sea.
I took pictures of your butt with my phone.

I should probably delete them
which makes me not want to.
It looks good in the window.
I think I'm gonna buy that,
Juno's peacock screamed.

4. My Future Children Who Don't Exist (That Makes It Seem Like They Might – Well, Who Knows? We Don't Want Them Right Now Though We Can Always Change Our Minds)

I get my legs from my daddy
and my heart from the lady
he wed. It's feminine but even
like a knife in the garter.
Astronaut, I'm your Houston.
I hear space-time's a language
we read until we're dead.
But what I really mean is fuck that.

Take all night,
half past five, drive it right down
like an owl through a sandstorm
headed west to some California.
There's this feeling getting scarcer
than a fragrance the wind's gotten to,
milling on the plains, arms up, lights out –
I can't help but feel a little Don Quixote.

What's that line?
Life's the play we play
like for real for real
or it's for keeps
that we did it.
Which simile lasts longer?

I smell like ice in June.
I look like a mirror in the picture.

5. The Highway at My Door

If Homer had a watch, he couldn't look at it.
Homer's watch is a sundial that conducts heat.
Homer's watch is his blind face.
Homer is like this clock with a body
or else just the idea of a person we made.

They say Homer won his blind audition
when they tested him behind the veil
so that he really could just be anyone.
This is the voice.
This is the voice of the war

come to tell you to come to war
with a smile and a T-shirt gun.
When we made potato cannons
in the backwoods of Tennessee,
the internet told us both how and why not to.

6. A Nest of Stares by My Window

I remember seeing two kids on the news who
went into the Toronto sewers in the early nineties
looking to meet up with the Teenage
Mutant Ninja Turtles and maybe did that
but didn't come back. Who would

either way? Some dreams you keep.
Others keep you. Like a book can
do that, even if it's on the internet
and only referenced as something
that influenced the next gen like a hand

influences its surroundings, touchingly
via gesture. There are smaller things
in everything until there aren't.
Once you go into them
you're like there forever

or until someone finds you.
At least ten things rise from the spring in spring.
Water mostly. Whatever, water,
I'm going to drink you if you don't tell me
where you go or what will come of you.

7. I See Clouds of Hatred and of the Globe's Fullness and of the Coming Emptiness

Ever since I quit smoking, I feel like I haven't.
I thought about accidentally stopping traffic
briefly, to tell everyone how hard it is,
which is an embarrassing feeling
like how being stupid is hard,
though you get the benefit of not always noticing
that you caused this thing that you want
more than a clock wants the minutes

to be a signal that evaporates like –
exactly what I should stop thinking about.
Smoke drifts up to the mirror and looks
older or pretty or alarming or truthful
or pitiable or pliant or whispery, like it's
whispering some idea put just under
the physical world of tasks we separate from
as to perform an escape. A lesson in aging

gracefully is not to be found here. We shook
like a wet animal a lot. Our prophets said
it was them who made us. Mayakovsky,
put your good leg down on one side and
your bad one on another. Mostly, I want to ride
like a Russian straddling a Russian cloud.
Shh, what was he saying inside all this time?
Be faithful to your most legible insanity?

Well, now you've gone and done it again.
M.'s dead, and he left his pants behind
on that cloud. Yes, the one that looks like you
if you were a person and not the second-person,
if you couldn't be used in a sentence.
In this human system that composes me
like a drunk Beethoven, I can be your Mountie.
Red suit, buckles up, let me guard you

from this world's lack of chivalry by filling it
with chivalrous actions, if you don't mind.
When we mindmeld it reminds me of the world,
also of a self-sustaining biodome of us.
Buckminster Fuller was my favourite human wizard.
In the future, there will be the future
and then that again. The past and I can't control
our having been a witness to this fact.

2020

I.

Two thousand and twenty is the arbitrary number
time's counted up to. There's more to see,
but she stopped for a year to think by the water.
What's the difference between beach music
and Bach? It depends on what you're wearing.
Barely anything is the perfect look.
I keep thinking you said something else.
What's your favourite skin-care destination?

Your granddaughter's name is Verizon.
She was in that beautiful TV show.
It is an anonymous runway tonight.
Sometimes when I go out onto it
I want to distinguish myself like how
I wish I could turn on my italics
but in real life, really leaning in, like
I'm a good listener with bad hearing.

My eyes are bigger than my hands can sow.
Do you think I should do something about that?
Maybe there are mandrakes after all,
though they're all dead or liminally
existent like an advertiser in the garden
branding the roses. Make it rain
cash like petals on a wet black bough.

I dreamt I was at a Korean spa in Rio.
I think a gnat just went into my eye on purpose.
Dragons are so in right now.
We got pierced in a secret place called:
The Mall. Protest is an adaptive response
to how killing someone is like yelling forever.
Suddenly all I can think about is one direction:
up, and how things should always go that way.
Like a plant, my concealed weapon is time.

I need you to balance my power systems.
I want you to meet the vegetable I invented.
This vine-jewel emits as from a godly source:
the backyard. Its properties of alchemy include
minor fruit-necromancy, satanic doodlings,
and a deadly poison. Americans are immune
to it via a ghost vitamin the founding fathers
deliver to them daily in an old version of light.

FACT: American sunlight is strongest in Puerto Rico.
FACT: Eve's apple was probably a tomato. Leave it
there, like a delight, and then return, young pilgrim,
only to find it again, laid out: what the Sun made
with its helpers. Nature's a bad baker. Everything's
about distribution. My name's Monsanto, and I'm post-
Earth. I live mostly on the moon and in St. Louis.
I guess that makes me bi-spherical.

2.

A wing makes these parts of flying:
a shining web, a floating ribbon of milk.
A mother makes these parts of life like
a god makes being a badass its thing.
Here's your elevator and its attendant opening
out into the penthouse of basic existence.
They ain't paying you to drink, Krishna,
but it's do or die. *I absorbed her entire life force
in self-defence.* The whole thing's written
except for this part that you can actually see.

3.

I left my golden bell somewhere,
probably among all these pomegranates.
Your hair is so good right now, Persephone.
I hear there's a temple in your locks that
you have to be a shampoo to get into.
The myth of you is stuck on repeat.
The underworld is an animated .gif
of something the world makes up here.
Zeus is most definitely an asshole.
Weather only bought a timeshare.

Your mom ran around the Earth with torches
like if the whole Olympics were a mother.
Hades wants a nondisclosure agreement.
There are these seeds that grow into time,
months of it, and then you get out of Hell
like a bad situation. Girl, both hit it and quit it.
I think this is a superfood. Sayat-Nova,
I name you the emperor of naming
the colour of things exactly as they are,
so what's red in the complete dark?

There's this strange root that's dug in.
Glow like a fat bug, nocturnal plant. Say:
I like the pageantry of when they bring us up
from the ground and say, *I see you there,*
not what you are the root of, the way colour

makes things seen, as if from nothing.
Night vision is like having visions.
My eye cones are filled with the moon.
Bats make things seen to sound. I'm wearing
an LBD to the party. Basic or not, I'm well-lit.

4.

I move around a lot, but I'm mostly from the sea.
Heaven sent its messengers again.
You're the Frank to my Ocean, you are
the sea of fruit to my sea of water.

5.

The temperature of yellow can affect you.
Taste's turned into this turning over of
the exact thing you encountered at the beach.
They built bunkers underneath paradise.
If fruit could bear arms, this apple's packing.

Everyone is here. There is a feathering
that pineapple does to flavour.
It's like burying a time capsule
and opening it simultaneously
just to mark the new New Year.

Maybe Neptune invented the Kraken
as a kind of pre-emptive sculpture.
Medusa gives good face. Ice makes
walking hard but walking on water pretty easy.
That's only one way to be a god.

Make the rain into a complicated Nebbiolo
and drink it with your friends. Like everything,
tax the rich, pool our resources, learn to swim,
maybe forget how to be a god sometimes,
and then, sometimes, make everything stop.

6.

The magician's under the blanket.
Your delicate ear is carefully garlanded.
The sage is on fire, is the message
the sage being on fire signals to you
in smoke, like how smoke can signal
a word like *smoke*. What happened
to Florida? Let's be in touch wherever.
Whatever happens, you need to grow up
from the earth and shake flavour out from under
its green cushion. Woodfeather, what wound bird
unwound its spool into what leaf-thing you are?
It was Sage with her wide eyes in the herbarium.
Sage the Gemini knows she's going to shake it
like a green bell. Sage draws beautiful things
like a printmaker. Sage draws evil spirits
from the body. Lana Del Rey's mystery illness
is that she's made of money. I want to be as naked as
Johnny Cash in a pile of cash in heaven in spring.

THE RED CARPET STEP AND REPEAT

I hate winter because it's not spring
which is like a smaller version of summer
when things actually happen and when
you'd like to stay in, like in a picture of you
in winter on a card that explains what happened
to the year to your whole family. I can't wait
for summer until I accidentally do wait for it
to happen, and it does, like how death does.

YOUTH AND AGE

I don't know about you,
but I'm feeling 222.
If I were a guest judge,
I'd marry you live.

I hated my haters bc
I was too young
to check them out in pity
at the afterparty door.

THE NEW FACES

There's new, and then there's the all-new you, young as an
opening note.

I wrote you in song.

So you'd hear me.

What weren't you doing at the Awards tonight?

I'm listening in, in the studio.

The beats we made keep beating.

A producer has only this one heart.

Music never listens when you tell it to stop.

A PRAYER FOR MY DOG

I wish the strongest ghost were here
to guard my Brooklyn baby
from whatever things are
until it's all just easier thoughts
like breakfast. Make sure
my bodyguard guardian angel's packing.
I don't want to have to mourn on the internet.
If I were in the post-apocalypse,

I'd do a lot of worrying.
What else? I'd plant a tree.
I'd change my name to Merlin,
hunt wild game in an abandoned Target,
then die of something lame
like dehydration or death.
Everything's an everyday thing
every day. Your favourite weapon

is also the katana. I don't think
people want to see
a movie about my life,
but maybe a poem,
if that's something you can look at
with whichever eyes look in language.
I missed my dog, so I wrote her.
Dear Laura Dern,

Dear deer in the way in the snow,
when I'm travelling through the dark
like a proper samurai, because of you
I don't wear loud shoes anymore.
When dogs die I feel old.
People expect you to set an example.
Some people light roses on fire
in Photoshop. I don't know any trees I want to be.

TWO SONGS FROM A PLAYLIST

I.

Talking to the dead is better when you're talking
to the dead to yourself. There's less in the way.
Here we are together, and no one else.
Now I can really let down my hair, to you,
Prince, at the bottom, formerly known as
what wasn't climbing up to get me. My post
ain't permanent, but I need a permanent rescue,
that and you reincarnated back from the nineties.

I've jammed out to your songs in my car.
I perform ska as a defence mechanism.
I'm just a girl, but that's not a real thing.
I love your uniqueness. You really touched me
in my life. I know Courtney Love was right.
I don't know how to describe this reality
sport: cheerleaders consider the inevitability
of aging. They think you can win this battle.

2.

I'm tired of how humans can be
sad as snow accountants
in their digital blizzards.
Alarm me like a Miley
with her free starlight,
delivered in the latest way. Say,
Look what I've found: this
never-before-seen life form.

Every one of your contacts
touched you some moment or way.
Which love emoji is your favourite?
Is it the one that's a face in love?
Do you recognize love as a conflict
of interest? Plaintiffs always go first.
Tell me the object that first comes to mind
when I say something's on fire is your heart.

FRAGMENTS

1.

Out of Mac Miller's mouth: get faded,
then play the maestro. Out of the wind:
a voicebox in a vacuum. Out of nothing:
repeat after me after me.

2.

Anything that you get done leaves an effect,
but its main effect is that you can't go back
before anything. I guess an action like going
out to L.A. can be like being Columbus
getting into the new world without any ID
'cept some dimples and shorty's whole 'tude.

LEDA AND THE SWAN

Like a gun: the wings kept going off
above this whole situation of thighs
and webbed feet, a neck, and another
longer, feathered neck; fuck grace,

this is gross. Fuck Zeus.
He isn't boyfriend material
even, and maybe especially, as a swan.
Thank God I'm not a Greek god.

They call me Lady Leda.
I know that bird's a playa.
Like a feather tornado,
he chased me a la playa.

Don't worry about that god, age sixty-nine, found dead
in his jail cell. Did she put on his power
before the indifferent beat let her drop?

ON A PICTURE OF A COWBOY BY
RON TARVER

You're riding through Philly in 1993 in a museum —
red shutters, white brick. You put on a white hat,
you make a decision. Unwearied eyes upon pigs,
nobody is fitter to keep watch than you, cowboy.
Philadelphia loves being alive and freedom and wild
horses. Wild horses, they live in a few wild places.
Wild horses never dragged nothing. I loved you
better than my soul. I forgot how far Saturn is.
I forgot how many moons it has. Seven times you
is a place. Into your fourteen arms, the police nuzzle
their little deer mouths. Dear mouths of the police,
say there is an apology in a circular letter immediately
to be read, if possible, everywhere. I keep watching
you through your bodycam. Though I can't see you,
or sometimes you're just a hand, I know where you go.
Stand down. My poetry can be so white. FTP.

AMONG SCHOOL CHILDREN

1.

I went to school so many times
I can't count, though I learned how to
while I was there. There, I said it:
I'm tired of learning in the old ways again.
I studied like a student. I teach like a guy
who goes by the name of *Teach*.
I've stopped thinking in lessons.
They say you need a licence to preach.

2.

Wait, no, they just say, *Preach*.
Everything you are good at is listening.
Everyone you are good to can see.
Every day I meet you it's today again.
Every time I want to's right now.
My tattoo is like an ad for California.
J. has these bones drawn on his bones.
Fuck money. I want your *Mona Lisa*.

3.

I dreamt I was in the nuclear holocaust
again, except this time I'm co-bunkered
with Martha Stewart. She makes everything,

including my day, even makes it look easy
to get out of prison and survive whatever
destructions. Almost anything can be a shiv.
That's what I learned like a schoolboy
fresh out of school as a summer in June.

4.

I pledge myself to this beauty
like I never had shit, because
I never did until this reasonably
functioning education system
elucidated this fact to me in language:
critical thinking is the means by which
one is able to do more than feeling
this feeling of everything all at once.

5.

Finally we're people, carefully.
Don't throw the baby anywhere.
Separate the water from its bath.
Cows can't read but neither can horses,
in this way that makes it cool to be
illiterate (in their horse-wildnesses.)
Most of the old gods hated books.
They were too busy transforming.

6.

Plato thought a lot of things twice
the way looking suggests one thing
before that thing starts to move.
It's not like you can turn off a window.
If I were a team of swimmers, I'd want to be
controlled by a hive mind like Socrates's.
I needed a whole life to ponder what it is
I get for free, so they gave me one.

7.

Sometimes all I know for sure is: I love movies.
Die harder than vengeance dies in heaven.
Die harder than the four horsemen can kill.
I'm talking to the thing that is death.
Work like a flower. Run like a bear would,
toward you, if you tried to outrun a bear.
I feel like a thought experiment a lot.
It's about being a sequel to yourself.

8.

Beauty doesn't happen on its own.
There are all these accomplices.
Make it misty. You can have half for free.
Here I am where I am an astonished man.
I am an astonished man for once.

Here by you, I'm being astonished
by how the stars are and how
suddenly everything twerks.

SHOUTOUT TO MARS

Who's that man who's gotten into my planet?
Check him out twice and return him with a late fee.
I take my wine black. I take the line back.
This place congratulates you just for being you
in it. Ain't it called a colony for a reason?
Something about us being aliens together.
This boy could drown you in the ound
of deaf nightingales given the chance.

Oedipus is Narcissus's sister.
Life's a system of instances.
Fate's a bird that's been fucked with
like a schedule on the tarmac. Delta,
you owe the flightless an apology.
Like a rover on Mars with an off-wheel,
I spin in a circle and spit. Space is
as good a place as any for cowboys.

I've stumbled into gardens more majestic
than nature. When I was God, I was
constantly naked. On yonder hills they built
my gym. My mermaid wants to be a land animal.
Like a bad seed in good land we'll root
for the home team, this burden of possibility
like a feather jacket. I'm still at the harbour
waving my hanky like I was at farewell.

I read William the same way I read Emily.
I mean to say that I sightread them.
What does a flame have to do anyway
to be governmentally designated as
an eternal flame and thus eternally
protected from all forms of snuffage?
Light is not an employee of the state.
Everything is horses here, even the sea.

EMOTIONAL INTEL

The difficulty of everything is always there.

Staying hard is a way of staying easy.

Weather is a full-body bodysuit.

I'm glad I'm not water in outer space.

Crystals are what weather looks like on the inside.

I want to be locked in the museum overnight in a way
that I now realize is erotic.

I'm as lost in the archive as the archive.

If you look hard enough, things move, and it's like you
made them do that.

Try you, for example, and you will, though the reason
that's true is still incommunicado as an avocado.

I place my seed on the windowsill.

When it sprouts, I place it in the wild.

Everything changes everything.

You can hit the jackpot from behind.

Can I turn the light off?

Hold on, where's my phone?

Look something up.

THE FOOL BY THE ROADSIDE

When you have worked
in the future of being
and in this future of being
a dead thing after that,
there you'll go returning
lost strings to their lost quartet.

Where'd you go when you kept going
out in all this time this time?
A road can be a bad place for running.
I'm more of a hitchhiker than a hiker.
This highway is historic
like us to the future.

MERCE CUNNINGHAM AND HIS DANCERS

1.

It's weird that my heart has literally gone
crazy. I want to write a bestseller called *You*.
The Magician's assistant is sometimes a broom
and sometimes anything else that exists in the world

that can turn into a floating version of itself.
Devil, be advised, it's cold up here
on Earth. Put down your ray-gun, Raymond,
everyone could never love you at once.

I feel like one of the many Will Smiths
in this world who is not Will Smith,
father to Jayden and Willow,
just trying to make it out alive.

2.

Independence Day will actually happen
in the future, again and again.
Alien race, race me down the beach.
One-man causes aren't un-American.

My man causes the ocean to exist –
which is to say the ocean and all of its extensions
in thought and beauty, which isn't a thought,
or, well, I keep thinking this same thing

about movement, how dance is that just
altered by a basic wish. I want to be
a Buddhist in the basilica, a priest
in the casino, or a dog at the zoo.

A MAN YOUNG AND OLD

1. New Moon

It was tried thoroughly as a moon
can be tested for life – yes,
we even found water. Whatever
murderous bird nested its golden egg
here, poised atop a marble bridge,
that's been slipped into the gorge

the moment a wind bore itself
suddenly enough to purchase
this whole life at its going rate,
has flown off. I pick my flowers
like a gorilla lost in the roses.
That pond is full of the dead

insects of summer being eaten
by this nuisance of pollywogs.
There had to be a decision to
make any decision first before
a decision could take place.
At the point of no return, we meandered.

2. Human Dignity

A rock is as dumb as a planet.
Why don't people just say what they mean?
PERSON 1: How are you?
PERSON 2: I'm dying.
Then the person does die
and doesn't say a thing.

Now what? said me and the moon.
Because I have a phone, I looked at it.
What did you do? I hear you did life.
What's there to surrender but love?
I misplaced my original question.
Is this your human dignity or mine?

3. The Mermaid

This one time a mermaid
fell in love with some guy
and took him to her mer-
queendom accidentally
or not accidentally except how
then he drowned.

4. The Death of the Hare

I ate rabbit happily.
You made it happily.
Nothing killed it but luck.
I want to go hunting with my dog
and never catch anything
but find stuff like bats

and bark at them. I guess
I don't really want to be a dog,
with their commendable traits,
but if I were one I'd be yours.
Being a human has this inherence:
this having to be a human being.

5. The Empty Cup

Mountain Dew was named after a poem
of ancient nature called 'Mountain Dew.'
I'd drink it, says the drink to its drinker.
Me too, says the thought to its thinker.
I want to plant water in the ground
like a fountain. Call the plumber.
No, call the fountain engineer.
My favourite ancient polymath
steampunk water-clockmaker is
al-Jazari. He designed an infinite flute.

6. His Memories

We already did this.
We already did do this.
We did this thing once
already when we were
doing this thing we were
doing. We don't remember

things. We don't remember
things, us being memories.
I'm not a morning person,
because I am the morning.
Memory is a bad currency.
I'm always losing you, money.

I'm like money in the way I'm spent.
I go first before I go to the end.
Win the lottery and cash out in jewels.
Remember how we brought the gods
back just to take their pictures? I forgot
we were real as a defence mechanism.

7. The Friends of His Youth

All my jokes went inside.
I love at least two Jessicas,
but possibly all of them who exist.
Jessica Alba, I don't know you that well,
but I'm open to the possibility of our friendship.
I used to lie around getting stoned making blogs
dedicated to obscenely depicted .gifs.
I made this one in which you emerge like a twinkle
in your own eye, again and again, I guess forever.
Like a TV lost in a hospital, it keeps playing.
It's rush hour somewhere. Everywhere,

my spatial recognition is off.
That square opened up into the whole world.
¿Barcelona, cómo te va allí?
I hear you go slowly into the gay sunrise.
The times fit into one Apple watch.
Now I want to think of sentences
you can read but all at once
on a small screen like: *Go.*

8. Summer and Spring

We sat in the vintage lawn chairs
drunk enough to shout about that
time you were lit flatteringly by an
active volcano. I figured something
out. That figures. I keep looking for
murderers in the blossom. I guess
summer is hot. That's why her name
is Summer. Like almonds, she's from
Cali. Tyler the Creator, bombarded by
yellow flowers, you're too fucking young
forever. *What water? Oh, that water?*
said the mountains. You can have it.
The history of sugar's disturbing.
Sweetness is a dark power.
Let's fix someone's problem today
then do that again tomorrow.

9. The Secrets of the Old

I once had a rendezvous when I was nineteen.
It was in 1944, and I was just drafted
for the war. It really has been a lot
of emails since then. I think it'll be good
to see him again. What's seventy years
made of? I thought I'd know by now.

If I sound off long enough
the general will notice me
and provide orders.
I've already got plenty
but not just one: first things
first. Then what's next.

Like an Amish horse, I never looked up
how to eat an apple, I just shook the tree.
One-man causes aren't not American.
Beauty isn't a thought, or, wait –
because if it were possible to think beautifully
what else is there but trying to do that forever?

10. His Wildness

St. Petersburg turned into a beach town
as soon as it got to America.
Nabokov wasn't ready for Florida
with its swarms of butterflies.
When you search for Russia,
don't be surprised if you find it.

History makes everyone famous
just for having lived through it.
Later we can go to the butterfly house,
suggested a child standing next to me.
I thought houses were made to house
whoever or whichever animal built them.

11. from *Idiots at Home*

I've never drawn up a beam myself. There are
so many empty buildings here. They beamed Spock back.
They built a house in a museum that burnt down.

The house was still there as an idea in the ashes.
I should only write my poems etched in sand
in glass blocks sold on the beachside for ten dollars.

There's a second gold rush happening in Alaska.
Fly-fishing is more a reason to be gay
in the wilderness than a sporting industry.

Gold is heavier than pot. You just need a little pouch
and a couple of months to vacay at a B&B
raking the silt at the edge of the Bering Sea.

A FEW MONUMENTS

Animals, which include humans,
should have a means to keep
their whole existence as naturally
as time burns its green library,
until all this knowledge, perhaps
gathered on purpose, might accidentally
cause, in part, a permanent animal
that's always there in the archive. Call it
a trace. Call the future bloodhounds
on the case. You can't burn down a song
just all the halls we sang and ran in.

THE GIFT OF MUNTADHAR AL-ZAIDI

Qusta ibn Luqa wrote about pollution
first in Baghdad in the ninth century.
We always wanted air to breathe.
This is a farewell kiss from the Iraqi people,
you dog, you say
                          as you throw the first shoe.
It's natural. The second seconds the act.
Both feet have to want to run. Some burning
bush spread a fire. Some painter spilled blood
blooming rose in an oil slick, flammably red
as Satan in a Texan church. The basket
went out. Existence's a conflict of interest.
Oil money's money. Luckily people ain't.
If money's paper (hint: it's not), we're trees.
We gave the years numbers
to track a flood. Years needed
a mother. Time burns like a shower
getting hot as your boyfriends flush.
Give the embroidered stars some space.
Stitches need air to heal.
                          Cut to that feeling –
Sappho sung it first – of us as the separation
of words from the body, this love letter left
on the air, that fragment left on the volcano
like a hand wandered away from its wrist,
its mind, ash-frozen in Pompeii in part.
In the event of a fire, take off your shirt

and throw it in. Eventually this message
will find the right you in y'all. Remember how
Saddam Hussein's son shot those dancers?
Which of the millions dead never danced?
This way is this one way. I wanted all of them
like Dr. Manhattan in an egg. *Cheer up.*
On the way to a funeral in Jersey,
'Alegría' plays on the car radio.
I love someone else's happiness.
Spring changed me into a bride.
That heart-stuttered look that love thought up
to make my eyes want to continue to look
at what is a destination called the surface
of your busy and perpetually moving body
stops me and other things from happening.
Let's circle the Earth like a lost Roomba
cleaning the world until battery death.
Al-Khayzuran bint Atta told stories to live.
Scheherezade was a version of her self
risen from traffic into queendom
by intelligence, a superpower revealed
by a letter hidden in an old book.
Curious as George appears in a trance
FaceTiming Spiritus Mundi: *Gyres*
turn. That's nature, all this living and dying
in sync with two forces. Wings beat
down and up goes the slow flamingo
into a hurried blur, pink with food.
I'm rideless.

We had all these years.

Georgie Hyde-Lees described a whole
system of energy of time *overladen*
with itself, said the voice through herself
for her bf to write down and know a spirit: us.
Love's no snitch, unless there's a love story
to tell to know to not stop to listen to time.
The wind never tells you what you want,
but what you need? That's a different take
made in lessons from your closest medium,
at the foot of the bed, levitating like a cloth
with a hand under it. I wanted to say
we are in the seat of fortune,

                               but we are
in fortune's backseat. It is an honour to be us
humans burning down the Capitol if need be.
Being keeps being hard to do for most,
but I'm not here to tell you what you know.
Basically, there is a way to bless chaos.
Look at how bright a candle gets, windlessly.

Everything's to go, nothing's to stay.

You can't look too long, even if it's pretty small
and pretty like a thought that starts a fire.
Prophecies make the future happen.
Throw the shoe. Throw the other shoe.

What you can't do in words, just do.
Say something we didn't understand before.
I could use a new language to face
these ends. You are full of good ones.
It takes money to educate ignorants,
and they have it. Sell all of the stuff
for all of the Earth,

                     all of the time.
Have you been here? Clean water runs
out like milk for a bowl to feed a kitten.
What if the voice of the dead speaking
through my love's voice casually prophesies
the end? People keep it popping. You say:
Where did you put the remote?

                          You say:
The beginning started with the end
in sight – close enough to see it's pretty
like the pink line between the clouds/mountains
from the lookout. Dorian never painted.

                         Big Bird
died. Don't pluck me. I'm tired of them
killing people when they come too close.
My brother fixes eyes in Baghdad
in a place claimed by another place.
Did they take us apart scientifically?
It seems they just took us apart. The point
is getting back together. My favourite
democratic confederal state capital's Rojava.

My favourite new country's Bougainville.
Why isn't there an even older Kurdish one –
nascent purple flower fruited into thought?
It's dangerous to own a tape in a library
outside of Istanbul or anywhere: culture
when it sounds like a threat or a song.
Harry Styles sings music into a room
to be heard in the international ballroom
that's thought. We get ice cream
after the Climate Strike. Show me
around your boat that doesn't use gas
to get from one place to all the others.
The wind is always telling me to hop on.
Every time you get bucked, get backup.
You have a reason to be afraid of thunder.
Bulbs flash. Flowers too. Light likes us.
Looking is an art that saying cannot do.
M. wanted to be in a poem. He told me
violets are blue, so I believed him.
Violent cats drunk on moon under
something like a spell written into light,
does it matter that our souls got closer
to getting out? Every day I'm falconing.
I remember when there wasn't

                            a moon.
You walked around in the room
telling stories from the great beyond.
I couldn't tell if it was witchcraft,
or, if so, whose problem was that,

since peace is what comes next
either way? You told me a future
full of students who climb trees
to learn where the world goes:
up when your words mean more
than money can say, up when
you look up and forget what's up
has been pointing its new finger
at the new cause without answer.
All this humanly beauty's a storm
we tossed our sailboats around in –
a revolution starting revolutions.
Flags break where the wind pulls them
out of their knots. Rope-play
is one way to say:
                    Fold the night
when I'm drunk on my youth again.
Be on my side of the chiliagon.
Spheres contain a single infinity
each. Walking up to mountains
I wanted to introduce myself: *I am*
a borderless thing like you under
all that surface. I can see your lava
climbing the walls from their insides.
Harun al-Rashid built a library for wisdom
to live in, because wisdom's alive or dies.
You might know him from a thousand nights.
Zubaidah's grandpa started Baghdad. Love
started us. Is it frightening to sing a duet

with yourself in the future past?
Mouldering away on top of a boulder,
I kicked the stand out and started to run.
Luckily there was a hill to roll me down.
I have a name as I write.
Did you get my text? It said
This has never been written before.
Days have sex with other days, of course.
The inarticulate lives in its hold on me (also)
until the beauty of something beautiful makes
the day again. *I lose a lot. It's kind of my thing,*
says space to the force on the moon.
Not believing you're still alive, living feels more
ungiven. Thrown things drop. Thrones get sat on.
Overthrowing is better than underliving.
Make other people progress. I'll be
anxious as long as I'm young, so I guess
that makes me young forever. A boy,
perched on some window met me once
on the internet in our national history
pre-spring, stayed through time, moved
with me, moved back moving as a movie
about love which is all of them and us too.
I'm no philosopher, so I can give bad advice.
Forgive me to yourself if not to me.
Love strikes and uproots the world. You
have the light, then you don't have the light.
Maybe we're newer than we think we are.
We survived ourselves, so own what's next.

What can you see from the top of a tower
at midnight on a full moon? It's over
over there too just you can see
how over it is farther. Sirens
should sound for ambulances.
I can hear the men coming with their guns.

DÍA DE MUERTOS

Halloween stops at midnight, but we're still in costume,
as is the custom. I think of undressing you like a ghost
at the potter's wheel but alive. I settle for one button
and undo it. There is no threatener to the rich in beauty
except themselves and what else, except death,
or except deciding to enter into a setting imbued
with the potentiality that you could be mauled.
Break out of Wall Street broke as a bull
in a Chinatown lunch spot. I order congee.
I break down grass in each of my stomachs.

There is no death like death.
All these other kinds live.
We're all a little Britney inside.
That's how I'll come back.
I wish for you to tell me
what to do, dead genie.
I need a mind that doesn't stop thinking.
I just passed a store called *Today*.
One version of paradise alters
itself to fit out the gate.

Dead royalty's always been classy.
There's always help for a widow's son,
Prince Charming. Just ask.
Nobody knows what's good
for you, especially yourself. Hit the gas

and the brakes at once. Hit me
with a single white glove twice. I can see
the gun in the mirror.
Dying's so normal now.
Everybody's doing it.

I don't care what your name is, Candy,
Storm, Princess, Harley Quinn.
The grapes rotted in their cedar.
My drag name is The Moon.
Night is repetitive for a reason.
I'm just another ghost on ecstasy.
There's a clock face on the dance floor.
Spirit guide, where did you get to go?
No, let me guess: ancient Egypt,
ancient Rome, or humanity's future planet.

Seldomly, Earth fills me with whole
thoughts. I feel pulled up like papyrus
from the Nile. Write your number on the top
of my hand. I will count up to it. Let's do a deck
in the backyard this summer together.
I love great timing. The more you save,
the more you can do with what you saved
from the great fires. They call this a circle
when everything's the same distance from
the point – which means there is one.

Harps announce you like a new text from you.
Death appears as a sound at the window,
revving through the red light, mufflerlessly.
I used to shoot down helicopters in the jungle.
Was that a ghost who said that or was it me?
Whenever death happens, I'm like: *Again?*
When we went to see where Michael was shot
for the last time, we drove by a farmer's market
in Ferguson to get to the place where he died
in Ferguson which is to say in St. Louis.

King Louis is cast in bronze on a horse on a hill.
His gaze casts itself off to all of the coasts.
Joni Mitchell is sirening by the Niagara again,
drawn to the idea of sound pouring out hard
enough to roar. If I were made up of water,
which I am, I'd fall too. I'd listen at the banks
like bank tellers on a morning smoke break,
umbrellaless, straightforwardly huddling up
against their stone wall, as if good posture
could solve anything, or was it everything?

We went to the gay club dressed as the dead
on the day of the dead, because it's your birthday
and lost the couples costume contest
to a slutty pair of Brothers Mario.
If I had as much pride as St. Louis Pride
I'd be lions. The first birth I remember
was my guinea pig's in Tennessee. I remember it was

right after seeing *The Lion King*.
I want to absorb all of my creature comforts
and emerge into a greater creature.

I think of Mewtwo. I think of you too.
All the phones are going off in the room,
like a ghost called all of them at once.
This otherworldly prank means
the dead are drunk possibly forever.
Thanks for holding, just one moment,
it's going to be silence that you hear.
What an intoxicating dilemma:
the rush at which one is required to act
to realistically invent a brand new desire.

The crease of my laptop
pinches out a single thigh hair.
My heart is trying to kill me.
It's beating on the door.
It's like: Let me in.
My farm burnt down.
Now I raise dragons.
Fold your wings.
Unfold your wings.
Take me to the tower.

ACKNOWLEDGEMENTS

Thanks to the editors of the following publications where some of these poems previously appeared:

The Elephants: 'Meditations in Time of Disaster'; Fort Gondo Poetry Broadside Series: 'Emotional Intel'; *Gather Journal*: '2020'; *Matte*: 'Sailing to Byzantium Again'; Still: 'Among School Children'; *The Third Rail*: 'The Tower'

With love to Diana Arterian, Mary Jo Bang, Jessica Baran, Agnes Borinsky, Julian Brolaski, CAConrad, Jennifer Chang, Sharmila Cohen, Douglas Crase, Sage Dawson, Alex Dimitrov, Rita Dove, Danielle Dutton, Mike Fu, Sarah Gambito, Cathy Park Hong, Susan Howe, Lauren Hunter, Lucy Ives, Gaïana Joseph, Joseph Kaplan, Martha Kaplan, Matt Keegan, Wayne Koestenbaum, Jennifer Kronovet, James Lindsay, Cole Lu, Dorothea Lasky, Gregory Pardlo, Sally Wen Mao, Jessica Madison, Dawn Lundy Martin, Ted Mathys, Stephen Motika, Eileen Myles, Carl Phillips, Morgan Parker, Tommy Pico, Sarah Nicole Prickett, Ariana Reines, Edo Rosenblith, Thora Siemsen, Crystal Sikma, Rachel Stern, Mónica de la Torre, Xuan Juliana Wang, Alana Wilcox, Ian Williams, Rebecca Wolff, Charles Wright, Jenny Zhang

Paul Legault is the author of *The Madeleine Poems* (Omnidawn, 2010), *The Other Poems* (Fence, 2011), *The Emily Dickinson Reader: An English-to-English Translation of the Complete Poems of Emily Dickinson* (McSweeney's, 2012), *Self-Portrait in a Convex Mirror 2* (Fence, 2016), and *Lunch Poems 2* (Spork, 2018). He also co-edited *The Sonnets: Translating and Rewriting Shakespeare* (Nightboat, 2012).

Typeset in Adobe Caslon Pro.

Printed at the Coach House on bpNichol Lane in Toronto, Ontario, on Zephyr Antique Laid paper, which was manufactured, acid-free, in Saint-Jérôme, Quebec, from second-growth forests. This book was printed with vegetable-based ink on a 1973 Heidelberg KORD offset litho press. Its pages were folded on a Baumfolder, gathered by hand, bound on a Sulby Auto-Minabinda, and trimmed on a Polar single-knife cutter.

Edited for the press by Ian Williams
Designed by Alana Wilcox
Cover by Joseph Kaplan
Tarot card by Pamela Colman Smith, Rider-Waite tarot deck
Author photo by Rachel Stern

Coach House Books
80 bpNichol Lane
Toronto ON M5S 3J4
Canada

416 979 2217
800 367 6360

mail@chbooks.com
www.chbooks.com